Florentine
Lives of the Saints

Saint Patrick
with Prayers and Devotions

Edited by
Mark Etling

Regina Press

Nihil Obstat:	Reverend Robert O. Morrissey, J.C.D. Censor librorum March 24, 2003
Imprimatur:	Most Reverend William Murphy Bishop of Rockville Centre March 31, 2003

THE REGINA PRESS
10 Hub Drive
Melville, New York 11747

All rights reserved. No part of this publication may be reproduced or transmitted in any form or by any means, electronic or mechanical, including photocopying, recording, or any information storage and retrieval system, without permission in writing from the publishers.

© Copyright 2003 by The Regina Press

Florentine Collection™, All rights reserved worldwide.
Imported exclusively by Malco.

Printed in U.S.A.

ISBN: 0-88271-161-X

Introduction

*I*t is certainly not surprising that the word "saint" is derived from the Latin word for "holy." The saints are known to us, first and foremost, as men and women of outstanding holiness, who surrendered their lives to God in loving fidelity to His will. Whether they were mystics or missionaries, educators or apostles, popes or laypersons, we remember and honor them primarily for the quality of their spiritual lives.

Saint Patrick, for example, was a man of great holiness, who believed that God was with him at every moment. But he was also a profoundly *human* being – in his humility about his own gifts as a missionary; in his embarrassment over his lack of formal education; in the emotional strength he displayed in enduring the many hardships of life in Ireland.

This book about St. Patrick is written in that spirit. As we reflect on his life, as we pray for his intercession, we should remember that Patrick is a saint – a holy man – because he was so human.

The Life of St. Patrick

*H*ow frightening the sight must have been – a fleet of *currachs* (longboats) descending on the small village of Kilpatrick in Roman Britain, manned by barbarian Irish slave traders. The intentions of the Irish invaders were clear – they had come to capture as many of the villagers as possible and exile them to Ireland as slaves.

To make matters worse, Kilpatrick had been left defenseless by the Romans. By the early fifth century the Roman Empire was breaking up, and it no longer had the resources to protect the farflung regions of Britain. The city of Rome itself would be overrun by the Gothic chieftain Alaric in the year 410. Europe was about to enter the period that would come to be known as the Dark Ages.

One of the villagers of Kilpatrick was a young man named Patricius (Patrick). The sixteen-year-old was the son of Calpornius, a Roman citizen, well-to-do landholder, member of the district council and a deacon. Although he came from a family of Christians, and had been brought up as a Christian, young Patrick was not particularly religious.

Patrick was carried into slavery that day, along with hundreds of others from his village, to Ireland, a remote region outside the Roman Empire. He was put to work as a shepherd for a Druid high priest named Milchu.

Life was surely very hard for Patrick. He was underfed and left alone with his herd for long periods of time. The loneliness he endured could have broken his spirit – but it had the opposite effect. As he wrote in his *Confession*: "Every day I had to tend sheep, and many times a day I prayed – the love of God and His fear came to me more and more, and my faith was strengthened. And my spirit was moved so that in a single day I would say as many as a hundred prayers, and almost as many in the night, and this even when I was staying in the woods and on the mountains; and I used to get up for prayer before daylight, through snow, through frost, through rain, and I felt no harm, and there was no sloth in me – as I now see, because the spirit within me was then fervent." (Translation by Ludwig Bieler).

Patrick's faith in God would eventually lead to

his escape. In his *Confession* he wrote: "And there one night I heard in my sleep a voice saying to me: 'It is well that you fast, soon you will go to your own country.' And again, after a short while, I heard a voice saying to me: 'See, your ship is ready.' And it was not near, but at a distance of perhaps two hundred miles, and I had never been there, nor did I know a living soul there; and then I took to flight, and left the man with whom I had stayed for six years. And I went in the strength of God who directed my way to my good, and I feared nothing until I came to that ship." (Translated by Ludwig Bieler).

After his return, Patrick probably studied in one of the monasteries of Britain (although some authors claim he traveled to Gaul, or modern-day France). Then, after a period of several years, Patrick received yet another vision from God – a vision more surprising and certainly more unexpected than the first.

In his *Confession*, Patrick reported he experienced the vision repeatedly. Victoricus, a man whom Patrick had known during his enslavement, appeared to him in a dream. He handed Patrick a letter entitled *The Voice of the Irish*. When he read the title, Patrick heard voices saying to him, "Holy boy, we beg you to come and walk among us once more."

Patrick responded willingly and eagerly to God's call, even though Ireland was considered a dangerous mission. Pope St. Celestine had previously sent a bishop named Palladius to Ireland, but he had died there. Pope Celestine then offered the difficult assignment to Patrick, and he accepted it without hesitation. Before leaving, he was ordained a bishop so he could ordain priests. At that time Patrick was about 40 years old. He would live and work with the Irish for the remaining 30 or so years of his life.

"I dwell among Gentiles, in the midst of pagan barbarians, worshipers of idols, and of unclean things" he would write about his new mission. He set out first to visit his old master Milchu, and to pay his ransom. He stayed there to preach the Gospel to his former fellow slaves and captors.

Patrick was a humble man, painfully aware of his shortcomings, both real and imagined. For example, he was embarrassed by his perceived lack of formal education: "I blush and fear exceedingly to reveal my lack of education." And he did not consider his faith or his popularity matters about which he could boast. He would write in his *Confession*: "I am Patrick, a sinner, most unlearned, the least of all the faithful, and utterly despised by many."

Yet his humility did not make Patrick shy or reticent about the dangerous mission he had embraced. He felt the presence of God with him at all times, and he firmly believed that the Providence of God protected him from harm: "Tirelessly, I thank my God, who kept me faithful on the day I was tried, so that today I might offer to Him, the Lord Jesus Christ, the sacrifice of my soul. He saved me in all dangers and perils . . . So, whatever may come my way, good or bad, I equally tackle it, always giving thanks to my God." And on another occasion: "Daily I expect murder, fraud or captivity, but I fear none of these things because of the promises of heaven. I have cast myself into the hands of God Almighty who rules everywhere."

Patrick continued his work in the northeast part of Ireland and established his episcopal see in the village of Armagh. He concentrated his efforts on the tribal kings, believing that if he were able to convert the king, the people would also convert. As more and more kings became Christians, they entrusted their sons to Patrick for their education and formation. Eventually many of these sons would become monks.

Once he converted a number of people in a village he would build a church there. One of the new converts would be ordained a deacon, priest or bishop and be left in charge. It is recorded that Patrick ordained some 350 bishops in all. Sometimes the king would donate a site to Patrick for both a monastery and a church.

As successful as his ministry proved to be, however, Patrick was seemingly never far from danger. He wrote in his *Confession* that twelve times he and his companions were seized and carried off as captives, and that on one occasion he was put in chains, and his death was decreed.

He also faced formidable opposition from the Druids, an order of priests and teachers among the ancient Celts who advised the Irish kings, and who also practiced magic. Patrick believed that the power of God was greater than that of the Druids.

A story from a biographer of the late 600s describes Patrick challenging the Druids to a series of contests at Tara in which he and the Druids tried to outdo each other in working wonders. On the night of the Easter Vigil, Patrick lit a fire on the hill of Slane, in direct violation of a royal command that anyone lighting a fire before the king would be put to death. The king ordered Patrick to be seized, but Patrick cried out for his enemies to be scattered, and many of the king's men died. As a result the king came before Patrick on bended knee. The next day a Druid caused a dark fog to cover the land. Patrick told the Druid to make the fog disperse, but he was unable to do so. Patrick then prayed and the fog lifted.

Patrick even faced opposition from the Church. At one point the elders of the Christian Church in Britain sent a delegation to investigate his mission. Patrick wrote his autobiographical *Confession* late in life in response to this investigation. As usual, Patrick noted that he drew strength from God at this time: "Indeed He bore me up, though I was trampled underfoot in such a way. For although I was put down and shamed, not too much harm came to me."

After many years of success - and hardship - Patrick died around the year 460. He was buried in his adopted homeland of Ireland.

Before Patrick, there had never been an organized or concerted effort to evangelize outside the Roman Empire. This is because the people outside the Empire were considered barbarians, and therefore less than human. But Patrick, like Jesus, reached out to those excluded and considered outcasts by most people. By the end of his life, Ireland was almost completely Christian. Irish monks would continue his commitment by evangelizing the so-called barbarian lands of Scotland, northern England, and western Europe.

Patrick was the first person in history to speak out without reservation against slavery. He developed a hatred of slavery probably because of his own experience as a slave. In his *Letter to Coroticus,* he excommunicated a British chieftain for carrying some of Patrick's own converts into slavery. He wrote: "Ravenous wolves have gulped down the Lord's own flock which was flourishing in Ireland . . . The whole Church cries out and laments for its sons and daughters." Patrick wrote that Coroticus' deeds were "wicked, so horrible, so unutterable . . ." By the time of Patrick's death, or not long thereafter, the Irish slave trade ended forever.

Patrick's formidable legacy includes as well the beginnings of Celtic spirituality, with its belief in the intimate presence of God in the Church, in Sacred Scripture, in people and in the created world. In his love of God and his commitment to prayer, Patrick is the perfect embodiment of this uniquely Irish spirituality.

Prayers of St. Patrick

Lorica (Breastplate) of St. Patrick

I arise today
Through a mighty strength,
   the invocation of the Trinity,
Through a belief in the Threeness,
Through confession of the Oneness
   of the Creator of creation.

I arise today
Through the strength of Christ's birth
   and His baptism,
Through the strength of His crucifixion
   and His burial,
Through the strength of His resurrection
   and His ascension,
Through the strength of His descent for
   the judgment of doom.

I arise today
Through the strength of the love of cherubim,
In obedience of angels,
In service of archangels,

In the hope of resurrection to meet
   with reward,
In the prayers of patriarchs,
In preachings of the apostles,
In faiths of confessors,
In innocence of virgins,
In deeds of righteous men.

I arise today
Through the strength of heaven;
Light of the sun, Splendor of fire,
Speed of lightning,
Swiftness of the wind,
Depth of the sea, Stability of the earth,
Firmness of the rock.

I arise today
Through God's strength to pilot me;
God's might to uphold me,
God's wisdom to guide me,
God's eye to look before me,
God's ear to hear me,
God's word to speak for me,
God's hand to guard me,
God's way to lie before me,

God's shield to protect me,
God's hosts to save me
From the snares of the devil,
From temptations of vices,
From every one who desires me ill,
Afar and a near,
Alone or in a multitude.

I summon today all these powers
   between me and evil,
Against every cruel merciless power that
   opposes my body and soul,
Against incantations of false prophets,
Against black laws of pagandom,
Against false laws of heretics,
Against craft of idolatry,
Against spells of women and smiths
   and wizards,
Against every knowledge that corrupts
   humanity's body and soul.
Christ shield me today
Against poison, against burning,
Against drowning, against wounding,
So that reward may come to me
   in abundance.

Christ with me,
Christ before me,
Christ behind me,
Christ in me,
Christ beneath me,
Christ above me,
Christ on my right,
Christ on my left,
Christ when I lie down,
Christ when I sit down,
Christ in the heart of every person
　who thinks of me,
Christ in the mouth of every person
　who speaks of me,
Christ in the eye that sees me,
Christ in the ear that hears me.

I arise today
Through a mighty strength,
　the invocation of the Trinity,
Through a belief in the Threeness,
Through a confession of the Oneness
　of the Creator of creation.

Prayer for the Faithful by St. Patrick

May the Strength of God guide us.
May the Power of God preserve us.
May the Wisdom of God instruct us.
May the Hand of God protect us.
May the Way of God direct us.
May the Shield of God defend us.
May the Angels of God guard us -
Against the snares of the evil one.

May Christ be with us!
May Christ be before us!
May Christ be in us,
Christ be over all!
May Thy Grace, Lord
Always be ours,
This day, O Lord, and
   forevermore. Amen.

The Rule of Faith of the Trinity
(a creed of the ancient Celtic Church)

*B*ecause there is no other God, nor ever was, nor will be, than God the Father unbegotten, without beginning, from whom is all beginning, the Lord of the universe, as we have been taught; and His son Jesus Christ, whom we declare to have always been with the Father, spiritually and ineffably begotten by the Father before the beginning of the world, before all beginning; and by Him are made all things visible and invisible. He was made man, and, having defeated death, was received into heaven by the Father; and He hath given Him all power over all names in heaven, on earth, and under the earth, and every tongue shall confess to Him that Jesus Christ is Lord and God, in whom we believe, and whose advent we expect soon to be, judge of the living and the dead, who will render to every man according to his deeds; and He has poured forth upon us abundantly the Holy Spirit, the gift and pledge of immortality, who makes those who believe and obey sons of God and joint heirs with Christ;

and Him do we confess and adore, one God in the Trinity of the Holy Name.

St. Patrick's Slogan

Christ in the heart of every one
 who thinks of me.
Christ in the mouth of every one
 who speaks of me.
Christ in every eye that sees me.
Christ in every ear that hears me.

Prayers to St. Patrick

Prayer of the Church to St. Patrick

God our Father, You sent Saint Patrick to preach your glory to the people of Ireland. By the help of his prayers, may all Christians proclaim Your love to all people. Grant this through our Lord Jesus Christ, Your Son, who lives and reigns with You and the Holy Spirit, one God, forever and ever. Amen.

Prayer to St. Patrick, Patron of Ireland

Dear St. Patrick, in your humility you called yourself a sinner, but you became a most successful missionary and prompted countless pagans to follow the Savior. Many of their descendants in turn spread the Good News in numerous foreign lands. Through your powerful intercession with God, obtain the missionaries we need to continue the work you began. Amen.

Traditional Irish Blessing

May the road rise up to meet you,
May the wind be always at your back,
May the sun shine warm upon your face,
And the rains fall soft upon your fields.
And, until we meet again
May God hold you in the palm
  of His hand.

An Old Irish Prayer

Deep peace of the running waves to you.
Deep peace of the flowing air to you.
Deep peace of the smiling stars to you.
Deep peace of the quiet earth to you.
Deep peace of the Son of Peace to you.

Chaplet of St. Patrick

*P*rayer on the medal: The Apostles' Creed

On each of the twelve green beads:
　Pray one Glory Be, then:
Through the intercession of St. Patrick, may God Almighty strengthen my faith, and grant the grace of faith for others. Amen.

Concluding Prayer:

　*C*hrist as a light,
　Illumine and guide me!
　Christ as a shield,
　o'ershadow and cover me!
　Christ be under me!
　Christ be over me!
　Christ, be beside me,
　On the left hand and right!
　Christ be before me,
　behind me, about me;
　Christ this day
　be within and without me!

An Irish Blessing

May God grant you
For every storm, a rainbow
For every tear, a smile
For every care, a promise
And His blessings all the while.

May you live a long life full of
 gladness and health,
With a pocket full of gold as the least
 of your wealth.
May the dreams you hold dearest
 be those which come true,
The kindness you spread keep
 returning to you.
May the friendships you make be
 those which endure,
And all your gray clouds be
 small ones for sure.
And trusting in Him to Whom
 we all pray,
May a song fill your heart every
 step of the way.
May the love and protection

Jesus, His Mother and St. Patrick can give,
Be yours in abundance as long as you live.

The blessing of Mary and
   the blessing of God,
The blessing of the sun and
   the moon on their road,
Of the man in the east and
   the man in the west,
And my blessing with thee
   and be thou blest.

May you always have . . .
A sunbeam to warm you,
Good luck to charm you,
And a sheltering angel
So nothing can harm you.
Laughter to cheer you,
Faithful friends near you,
And whenever you pray . . .
Heaven to hear you.
May peace and joy surround you,
Contentment latch your door,
And happiness be with you now
And bless you evermore.

Irish Christmas Blessing

God bless the corners of your house and all
   the lintels blessed.
And bless the hearth and bless the board and
   bless each place of rest.
And bless each door that opens wide to
   strangers as to kin,
And bless each crystal window pane that lets
   the starlight in,
And bless the rooftop overhead and every
   sturdy wall.
The peace of man. The peace of God.
   With peace and love for all.

St. Patrick Novena

Opening prayer (each day):

*I*n the name of the Father, and of the Son, and of the Holy Spirit. Amen.
Come, Holy Spirit, fill the hearts of your faithful, and kindle in them the fire of Your love. Send forth Your Spirit, and they shall be created, and You shall renew the face of the earth.
*L*et us pray. O God, Who did instruct the hearts of Thy faithful by the light of the Holy Spirit, grant us in that same Spirit to be truly wise and ever to rejoice in His consolation, through Jesus Christ our Lord. Amen

Day One
Reading: Romans 2:17-25
Response: You know, and God knows, too, that I have lived among you since my youth in true faith and with a sincere heart. I have kept faith, and will always keep faith, even with the heathen tribes among whom I live. God knows I have neither cheated nor been false to any of them, nor even thought of doing so, for fear that I would cause them to attack God and His

Church, and to persecute all of us, and lest the name of the Lord be blasphemed because of me. For it is written: "Woe to the man through whom the name of the Lord is blasphemed."

Day Two
Reading: Ephesians 3:14-21
Response: For my shield this day I call:
   A mighty power:
   The Holy Trinity!
   Affirming threeness,
      confessing oneness
   In the making of all
      through Love . . .

Day Three
Reading: 1 Corinthians 2:10-16
Response: For my shield this day I call:
   Christ's power in His coming
   And in His baptizing,
   Christ's power in His dying
   On the cross, His arising
   From the tomb, His ascending;
   Christ's power in His coming
   For judgment and ending.

Day Four
Reading: Revelation 7:2-4;9-14
Response: For my shield this day I call;
   Strong power of the seraphim,
   With angels obeying
   And archangels attending,
   In glorious company
   Of the holy and risen ones,
   In the prayers of the ancestors,
   In visions prophetic,
   And commands apostolic,
   In the annals of witness,
   In virginal innocence,
   In the deeds of steadfast people.

Day Five
Reading: Daniel 3:52-90
Response: For my shield this day I call:
   Heaven's might,
   Sun's brightness,
      Moon's whiteness,
   Fire's glory,
      Lightning's swiftness,
   Wind's wildness, Ocean's depth,
   Earth's solidity, rock's immobility.

Day Six
Reading: Philippians 2:6-11
Response: This day I call to me:
  God's strength to direct me,
  God's power to sustain me,
  God's wisdom to guide me,
  God's vision to light me,
  God's ear to my hearing,
  God's word to my speaking,
  God's hand to uphold me,
  God's pathway before me,
  God's shield to protect me,
  God's legions to save me.

Day Seven
Reading: 1 Corinthians 15:35-44
Response: This day I call on all
  these heavenly powers to protect me;
  From snares of the demon
  From evil enticements
  From failings of nature
  From one person or many
  Who try to destroy me anear or afar.
  Around me I gather these forces
    to save my soul and my body

From dark powers that assail me:
Against false prophesyings,
Against pagan devisings,
Against heretical lying,
And false gods all around me.

Day Eight

Reading: Ephesians 1:15-23
Response: Be Christ this day my
    strong protector:
Christ beside me,
    Christ before me;
Christ behind me,
    Christ within me;
Christ beneath me,
    Christ above me;
Christ to the right of me,
Christ to the left of me;
Christ in my lying,
    my sitting, my rising;
Christ in the heart of all
    who know me,
Christ on the tongue of all
    who meet me,
Christ in the eye of all

who see me,
Christ in the ear of all
who hear me.

Day Nine

Reading: Psalm 33:1-13

Response: I give unwearying thanks to my God, who kept me faithful in the day of my trial, so that today I can offer to him confidently in sacrifice my life as a living victim to Christ my Lord, who preserved me from all my difficulties so that I can say as well, Who am I Lord, or what is my calling, since You have worked in me with such divine power so that today I should regularly exalt and glorify Your name wherever I happen to be not only when things go well, but also in troubles, so that whatever may happen to me whether good or bad, I am equally bound to accept it and always give thanks to God.

Closing Prayer (each day):

O great apostle of Ireland, and patron of our people, so many are indebted to you for the great treasure of our faith. Receive our fervent thanks for the zeal and charity that has been an invaluable source of blessings to so many of our brothers and sisters. We ask Your intercession for (*mention your intentions*); asking You to submit all our temporal and spiritual needs to God.

We pray, great St. Patrick, that we always be devoted and loyal; our thoughts be of Jesus; our hearts be His shrine, so that when our life's path has been trod, we may be found worthy of eternal salvation. We ask this through Jesus Christ, our Lord. Amen.